The Beadworkers Guild

INTRO...N
TO BE, ...ORK

Edited by:
Jill Devon and Liz Thornton

Bringing Beadworkers Together

The Beadworkers Guild aims to meet beaders' needs on different levels. From local meetings to international competitions, from learning how to do a particular stitch to discovering how and why other cultures use beadwork.

The editors would like to thank the following for their valuable contributions to the production of this book:
Isobelle Bunting, Gillian Lamb, Sue Maguire, Jan Newberry, Debra Ross and Alexandra Witney.
Illustrations and charts by Gillian Lamb and Liz Thornton
Photographs by Gavin Mist

Published by:
The Beadworkers Guild, P.O. Box 24922, London SE23 3WS

CONTENTS ◆◆◆◆◆◆

Introduction . . .

Welcome to The Beadworkers Guild Introduction To Beadwork Series. This series of books is designed to help you learn new stitches, give you beadwork confidence and inspire you to create your own masterpieces.

This first book in our series is all about bracelets. We think this is an ideal way to learn lots of techniques and sample new ideas. We have included all sorts of styles and many of the designs can be expanded to use as necklaces or braids and trimmings. So if you particularly like one, run with it and explore all the possibilities.

Use this book to its full potential; don't treat it like a library book (unless of course it is a library book!). Make notes and diagrams to help you where you think you may need to, write or draw ideas and bead small samples of each stitch in different colours and shapes of beads and stitch them to the page. This really will help you when designing projects at a later date. And if you need to magnify any of the charts and diagrams then take them along to your local photocopy shop to get them enlarged.

Use this book as a guide; we are not setting any rules – just offering ideas and handy tips. You will see from the different projects that we do not give you exact bead by bead instructions. Firstly we don't believe that is entirely possible – beads vary, people vary; and secondly, beading by numbers (as in other crafts) is really rather boring. What we want to see is you learning different stitches and techniques in a fun way so that when you have an idea you will know how to turn it into a reality. We want to give you the confidence to use your beads, to use colour and texture to create your own vision. You will discover that some stitches look really good in certain beads, and that some stitches work one way and not another. Then once you have mastered individual stitches you can try using them together; you will discover your personal preferences in stitches and in beads, but you will also learn to think "what if?"

This is our aim, for you to play and create. Do not be nervous.
If something goes wrong, and you don't like it, undo it and start again
(this is called the frog stitch – 'rip-it, rip-it'), and most of all,
ENJOY – Beadwork is not fattening!

How to use this book . . .

The projects in this book have been grouped into different stitches. We have done this so that you may see some of the possibilities available to you to develop your expertise and confidence within a particular stitch and on a small scale. We have included the most popular types of stitches and those that are appropriate for bracelets. We have not included loom work, since we think its potential is better developed on larger pieces. But we have included Daisy braids because they offer a whole range of surprising possibilities.

You do not have to work through the book stitch-by-stitch or project-by-project. Work with the ones you like the most, although it would be best to leave the freestyle designs (Peyote Pebble-dash and Ripples, Brick Mosaic and Coronet) and the Part 2 tubular stitch designs until you are confident with that particular stitch in its flat form.

The projects are aimed at both the beginner and the experienced beader. If you are a beginner, start with a project in Part 1 that appeals. Read how to tackle the stitch in The Techniques and refer to it as you go along.

If you are an experienced beader we hope you will enjoy the more freestyle designs, and that you will tackle some of the projects in stitches unfamiliar to you. Particularly, we hope that you can use our ideas and delightful photographs to give you inspiration.

Read through a project before you start it, and preferably before you buy the beads, so that you understand what it is you are about to do.

We have deliberately not been precise in our materials list. When we say 1 packet we mean a standard saleable quantity, generally 10g of seed beads, or 5g of Delica beads – that will give you more than enough. And when we say 'seed beads' without giving a particular size, we mean either size 10, 11 or 12 – whichever your supplier stocks.

For all projects, it is a good idea to consider the type of fastening you will use before you start – stitching on a bought clasp takes a lot less thread than making a beaded toggle. So leave a tail of thread which will be long enough to cope at the outset.

Similarly, always check the length of your bracelet, allowing for the fastening, before it's too late – making a bracelet that's too big to wear is a teensy bit annoying!

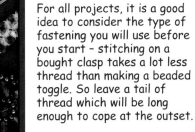

Materials & Equipment

You will of course, need needle and thread. Now it's quite possible to use any narrow-eyed needle and the first thread you can lay your hands on, but if you start off with the right equipment – and it really isn't much of an outlay, it will save you an enormous amount of frustration.

Beading needles have a flat eye to enable them to pass through small beads. (This means that round fibres are more difficult to thread in them than flat fibres.) There are various different sizes, with size 10 being the largest and easiest to thread. If you are going to pass through the bead several times (e.g. using square stitch), or will be using beads with a smaller hole then it would be advisable to use a size 13 needle. This is a finer needle with a finer eye, and is more difficult to thread. It will also go banana shaped pretty quickly and may also snap – so don't buy just one!

Nymo is a strong parallel-fibre nylon thread used originally in the upholstery industry. Being a flat fibre it is easier to thread through the beading needle. There are various thicknesses available, the most usual being B or D, which are both suitable for general use. D would be better to use where you need a little more strength, and B if you are passing through the bead several times, or if the beads have a smaller hole. Both come in a range of colours, which can be matched to your beads. Most useful are the neutral colours grey and beige.

Other most useful equipment would be very sharp small embroidery scissors and some very fine surgical tweezers – these are invaluable for removing knots, and for placing knots just where you want them!

Whether you condition your thread or not is largely a matter of personal preference. If you choose to do so then Thread Heaven is a very good silicon conditioner, smoothing and strengthening the fibres with a very fine coating, and a great improvement on beeswax. We would stress however that if you are using bugle (long) beads, or any other bead with a sharp edge that you protect your thread as much as possible by conditioning it.

When you have finished your work, a small (very small) dab of Fray Check or clear nail polish on the knot will secure it.

There are various suppliers of beads, and we have recommended several in the list on page 112. The size and shape that you choose will depend on your project, but there is a great variation between manufacturers, and even between the beads contained in one lot. If you are doing a project that requires even beads – flat, close-woven stitches – then try to buy all your requirements in one go from one manufacturer; your supplier should be able to advise you.

Be particularly careful when choosing bugle beads. They are, after all, cut glass, and many of the cheaper varieties have unpolished edges that will slice through your thread - all that work spoiled! Even in the better quality bugles you will get the occasional broken/sharp edge: throw it away! With misshapen seed beads you can utilise them in fringes, etc, but you will never find a suitable use for a broken bugle.

Different beads lend themselves to different techniques, but be careful when making 'bargain' buys. Cheaper seed beads are fine for netting and spiral and fringing, and when working freestyle, but for peyote and other close-woven pieces you will find that the better quality, more uniform seed beads or Delicas produce much better results.

If you're not sure what the difference between a seed bead and a Delica is, imagine the seed beads as little donuts- and when they are placed together the surface is bumpy and textural. Delicas on the other hand, are more like short tubes, and when they are placed together they slot in next to one another and create a more even finish. (Delica, by the way, is a trade name; other manufacturers call their beads Antiques or Magnificas, or Cylinders.) Conversely, if the stitch you are doing calls for the beads to sit at angles to one-another, then a seed bead will snuggle up close to its neighbours, and a Delica will give them the cold-shoulder.

All the beads, whatever their quality, have different finishes with varying degrees of permanence. Some dyed or galvanised finishes have a tendency to rub off, and many dyed beads can fade. Ask your supplier for advice.

A small tray lined with either velvet or chammy leather (in other words a dense-cut pile rather than a loop pile) is very useful to hold the beads you are working with and to stop them rolling around. And finally, and most essential of all, a good light to work in!

Tips

Due to the way the thread is wound onto the bobbin, it is easier to thread your needle from the Nymo bobbin before cutting.

Before you start, run your fingers tightly along the thread to ease the kinks out of it. If you wish to use a conditioner do so now, avoiding the needle area of the thread where the wax would clog the eye of the needle.

Periodically stop and allow your thread to unwind and then ease and condition it like you did at the beginning.

You might like to 'unwind and ease' yourself a bit too! Never bead for long periods at a time. It is so tempting to keep going, not realising how stiff you are becoming until you get up!

Do not think that you have to work every bead in your tray. Discard ones that are misshapen – if you are doing close, even work a bad bead will really show up, and make you wish you had not been so parsimonious.

Similarly, never re-use thread. Once kinked it will drive you mad by making knots all the time.

If, when working, you feel a knot forming, immediately loosen and remove it. Do not think it will go away if you ignore it, or worse still, disappear if you pull it tight- it will only get worse and leave you VERY FRUSTRATED! Once removed, ease the thread again.

You must be careful not to pierce the already worked thread with your needle. If you keep the tension even and always try to put the needle through the top of the bead hole the problem will be minimised.

Similarly, if you want to put the needle back through a bead to remove it, go eye first rather than point first.

Don't wait until the last minute to add a new thread. It's much easier to attach or weave in if there is plenty of thread to work with. It will save you endless minutes of frustration.

You will get the hang of how to hold your thread and work to achieve an even tension. Try holding the work between your forefinger and thumb, and wrap the working thread over the forefinger, holding it down with the middle finger, after each stitch.

3-BEAD NETTING

There are lots of different types of netting. You can work either top to bottom (vertical) or side to side (horizontal), and different numbers of bead in each net can create very different effects. It can be very open and lacy if more beads are used between each axis point, or, as we are using here, with 3 beads it can create a most lovely supple fabric, which is ideal for a bracelet.

With all types of netting it is a good idea to do some advance planning, and not just go where the mood takes you. The first row that you work sets the size of the piece and all the following rows will work off it. A design is more difficult to visualise than in some other stitches because of the arrangement of the beads. Use the 3-bead netting graph paper at the end of the book to help you.

One of the best things about netting is that it works very well with other stitches, either joining from them, or worked over them, and of course, you can have great fun embellishing on the top or inside the lacy weave.

Another point to remember is that your beads do not have to be of even quality for working in netting - they are allowed a little space to snuggle into their favoured position, and the more open you make your weave the more uneven they may be.

But for an elegant and practical fabric the tightest weave is 3 bead netting, so try it out with the following patterns, and then experiment . . .

Chequer & Chevron Cuffs

We've chosen two different designs – both follow exactly the same technique, you will just need to follow the relevant chart. You can make your cuff just as long as you want to by following the repeats (you could of course make it even longer, and wear it as a choker – how about adding a little fringe?).

There is a graph at the back of the book for you to create your own designs – we know you'll want to as this is the most satisfying and easy of stitches once you get the hang of it!

Materials (For either pattern)
4 packets of seed beads in different colours

Method:-

You will find the stitch instructions for 3-bead netting on page 98. When you are ready to start the cuff it is most important that you follow the pattern chart and mark off each set of beads as you complete them so you may wish to consider photocopying the pattern before you begin. Mark off the beads just strung to help you keep your place. Whilst working, remember constantly to check that you are following the pattern in the correct sequence, since a mistake would be very obvious.

There are 4 different colours in both these patterns; it is personal preference which one you choose for each section.

Thread on 27 beads in your main edge colour. Then thread up through bead no 21 to form a loop. Add 3 more beads and go up through bead no 17. Continue back to the top in this way and then you are ready to start the pattern. Always add 1 extra bead (E) top and bottom to form straight edge. Repeat the pattern as required. When your cuff is the desired length, work one row in the main edge colour, and then add a beaded toggle on one end and a loop on the other.

Experiment with:-
Patterns ◆ Colours

Chequer

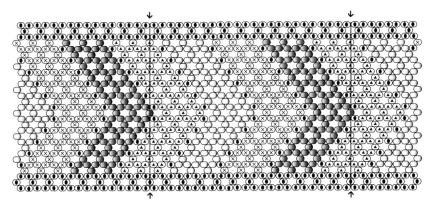

Chevron

PEYOTE STITCH

Peyote is a very popular stitch, very simple to do once you get started, and with many variations. We have included 7 projects for you - all lovely, and each producing a different effect. We have used several shapes of beads so that you can see how versatile this stitch is.

Peyote produces a tight, regular weave rather like a wall of bricks on its side. If you want to keep your piece so even that you may 'paint' a design on it in beads, then you really need to use Delicas that will sit together very snugly. If you are looking for an overall or geometric pattern then good quality, even, seed beads will give you a good effect. When you feel comfortable with the stitch you can try your hand at freestyle, and see the effect of using different shaped beads - we have included 2 designs that we think you will agree are very exciting.

Tension is very important when working this stitch - you must be careful to not make it too tight, which will make your finished work very stiff, but on the other hand if it is too loose it will not hold the correct pattern. Practise a little, and if you are starting this stitch from scratch, don't worry too much about your first few rows - you can always pull them out later and, if you want, rework them in the opposite direction when you have got your tension right.

Peyote can be worked in all manner of directions: – linear, tubular and circular. It can create ruffles and waves, it can be used to paint pictures, or closely cover objects. Look at these exciting projects in the photo and see what we mean . . .

The
Beadworkers
Guild

11

Electra

This is a nice introduction to peyote stitch being a very basic diagonal pattern. Start off by using either seed beads or Delicas, and once you have mastered the stitch, you could try using different shaped beads (such as Miyuki triangles) to create a more exotic and free form appearance. Keep your tension even, but not too tight or the cuff will not be supple.

Materials

2 packets of different coloured seed beads or Delicas

Method:-

Thread on 12 beads in your Main Colour (M). Pick up a further M bead and pass the needle back through the no 11 bead. Pick up 1M and pass the needle through no 9 bead. Continue until the end of the row. (The first 12 beads make up rows 1 & 2, and there are now 6 beads in a row.)

Add a further 2 rows in the M colour. (Total 5.)

Row 6: Pick up a Contrast bead (C), pass through the next bead, and pick up 1M and pass through the next bead. Repeat until the end of the row.

Rows 7, 8 and 9 repeat as Row 6.

Rows 10 – 13 are opposite – in other words start with M.

Rows 6 – 13 make up the pattern; you will see that at the edges of the cuff there are alternating pairs of beads of each colour. Continue until the bracelet is the desired length, and finish with 5 rows of M. Add a beaded toggle on one end and a loop on the other.

Experiment with:-

Colours ◆ Patterns ◆ Types and sizes of beads used

Two Tone Triangles

This is a very simple Peyote design, and you could use many different types of bead shapes, but we have used Toho Triangles (which are a much sharper shape) rather than Miyuki Triangles (which are a softer, bumpier shape). The very subtle shade effect is achieved by using a frosted and shiny version of the same colour. We have given this bracelet a little frilly picot edging and a beaded clasp to give it an added textural effect.

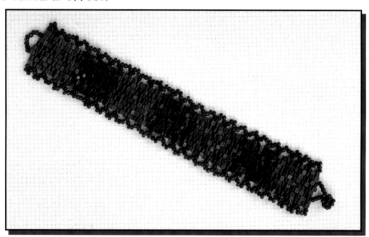

Materials
1 packet each of shiny & frosted metallic Toho Triangles, and seed beads to match

Method:-
Thread on 8 frosted beads. Using frosted beads, work backwards and forwards eighteen times, i.e., until you have twenty rows.

Continue working blocks of twenty rows, alternating between shiny and frosted beads, until there are seven blocks in all. Check the length with your wrist measurement. If you need a longer bracelet add more rows equally to either end.

Work a picot edge in seed beads down each long edge (for instructions see techniques). Make a beaded fastening at one end of the bracelet and a loop of beads to fit at the other.

Experiment with:-
Colours ◆ Types and sizes of beads ◆ Different edges

Basket Weave

This gorgeous design is made using the 2 Drop Peyote principle – the smaller beads are used in pairs as though they were a single bead. It utilises the Double-Delicas (Miyuki size 8 or Toho size 3.3) alternating with the 2 drop Delicas. The size ratio of this combination of beads works perfectly, but you could investigate some choices of your own. We have made ours very simply in just one subtle colour, but you could try all sorts of variations – with both colour and positioning of bead sizes.

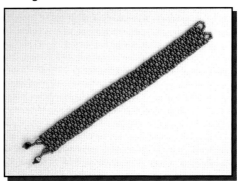

Materials
1 packet each of Delicas and Double Delicas

Method:-
Thread on 12 small beads. *Pick up one large bead, miss a pair of small beads and put the needle back through the next two small beads. Repeat twice to complete the row.

Pick up two small beads, miss a pair of small beads and put the needle through the next large bead. Repeat twice to complete the row.

Pick up two small beads, miss a large bead and put the needle through the next pair of small beads. (You may have to wiggle the point of your needle a little to get it in past the large bead.)

Repeat from * until the bracelet is the required length. Make two toggles for the fastening. Return to the beginning of the bracelet and make loops of beads to fit the toggles.

Experiment with:-
Colours ◆ Different placement patterns of beads ◆ Same pattern in brick stitch, which would give you different placement choice

Picket Fence

This is absolutely ideal if you're in a hurry to make something to wear for the same evening, and it can look so different, depending on whether you use glitzy beads as we have here, or dark and subtle. This would also look super made longer into a choker, possibly with a fringe addition. You can, of course, use any size bugle beads that you wish, but do thoroughly check and cull them before you start – some bugle beads can be quite horrible. You may also wish to put conditioner on your thread to give it a little added protection from those sharp edges.

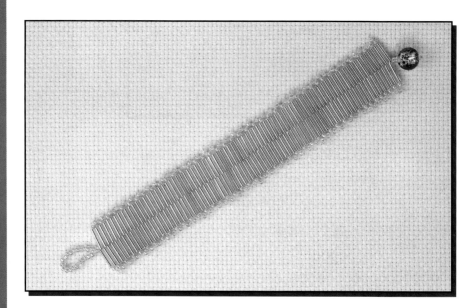

Materials
1 packet each of bugles and seed beads

Method:-
Start peyote stitch using just 2 bugle beads (in step 1 of the techniques). Only one bugle bead is picked up in each row.

When you have reached the desired length work a triangular picot edging along both sides (for instructions see techniques). Make a toggle of beads at one end and a loop to fit at the other.

Experiment with:-
Colours and finishes ◆ Fringing

Fig 1

Fig 2

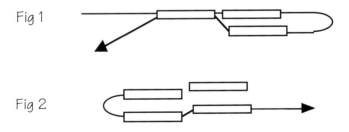

Star Spangled Bracelet

If you're itching to follow a 'proper pattern' we've put one in now for you, and what could be more fun than a take on the Star Spangled Banner – of course if you didn't do it in red, white and blue, then it would look completely different – why not try it in other colours?

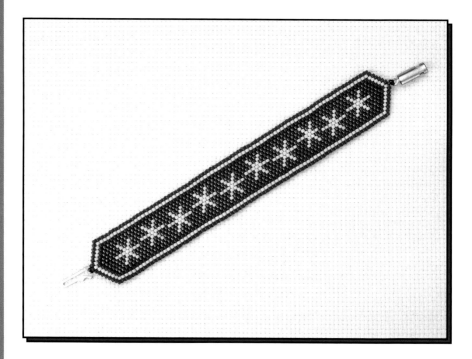

Materials

1 packet each red, white and blue Delica beads
Clasp

Method:-

This design is worked in Even-Count Peyote (16 beads wide) and therefore does not have a centre bead. The stars are placed offset by one bead to the left and then to the right, which gives a pretty effect.

Follow the chart until your bracelet is just short of the desired length. Decrease at each row by one bead either side, continuing to follow the pattern, until there is 1 bead left. Unthread your needle and repeat this at the other end. Check the size on your wrist, allowing for the clasp. If it is too long then remove rows equally. If it is too short then add rows of two beads equally. Attach a clasp.

Experiment with:-

Colours ◆ Graphing other designs in this stitch or other stitches (see Stars and Stripes in Square Stitch)

Treasure

We've put in a 'pattern' for this bracelet, because we do know it can be a bit daunting starting something completely different to what you're used to! But really the whole point of freestyle stitch pattern is to do your own thing! Firstly you need to decide on a colour range and collect your beads – we suggest 6 – 8 different types (e.g. Delicas, seeds size 8, size 11, hex, triangles feature beads, etc.). If you feel confident (and we're sure you will once you've done a few of the earlier patterns), then experiment, and enjoy collecting your treasures and playing with your beads!

Materials

6 – 8 different types of beads (Delicas, seeds, hex, triangles, etc)
Optional Feature bead for clasp

Method:-

Pick up 5 or 6 of each bead that you have set out. Thread sufficient beads to go roughly round your wrist, or slightly shorter – you can always add extra length later. It doesn't matter what order, just one that is pleasing to you. Make sure that if you are using beads with a large centre hole that the beads either side of this section do not slide into this central hole. Work at least 4 or 5 rows of peyote stitch, changing beads for each section as you go along.

Make at least 3 or 4 small peyote sections separately in either the same beads that you are using, or some different ones. The sections could be oblong, or square, or leaf shaped. Attach these to the peyote band on either edge, or layer them on top in the centre.

Embellish as much or as little as you like.

Adjust length to fit. Attach a loop at one end and a favourite bead, button or small beaded bead at the other.

Experiment with:-

Colours ◆ Types and sizes of beads used ◆ Different shapes and sizes of embellishments ◆ Different numbers of beads used

Fig 1

Fig 2

Fig 3

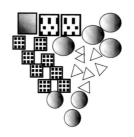

Fig 4

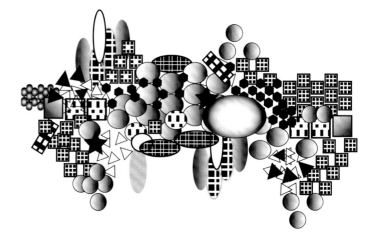

Ripples

This is a really terrific design, which is easy to do once you have mastered peyote stitch – it's basically lots of little triangular sections joined together. The beauty lies in your choice of beads – as you can see from our main example we have used a soft palette of beads with a subtle change of colour and texture. Make your own choice, remembering that the two ends of your bracelet are going to meet so your two end colours should be compatible! In the photograph here we have part of two more bracelets as examples of different bead choices – once you have got the idea of the main example, try your hand at one completely different, with triangles, squares, bugles, etc. We guarantee your friends will be truly impressed!

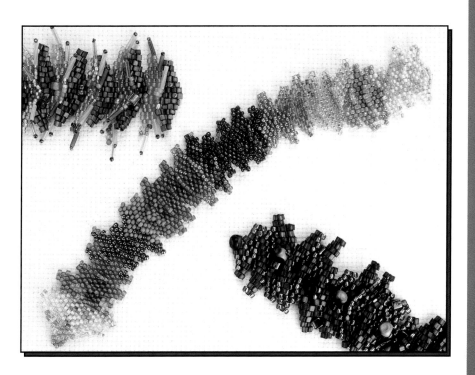

Materials

Oddments of different coloured seed beads (15-20 colours/finishes)
Magnetic clasp or make your own hidden clasp – see below (which will
require an inch or so of wire)

Method:-

Thread on 17 beads in one colour (Fig 1) and then continue in peyote
stitch (Figs 2 & 3) until you have 4 rows. On the fifth row turn by
following the thread path in Fig 4. This makes the decrease on this
side. Continue to peyote back to the other side – side a. (Fig 5).

Turn and decrease on side a. by following the thread path in Fig 6.
This makes the first decrease on side a. Continue to peyote back and
forth using the turn in Fig 6 to decrease at both sides.

When you have put in the final bead at the tip of the triangle, turn
once more so that the thread exits from the top bead and pass the
needle down through the next 3 edge beads, and pick up 5 beads (Fig
7) to start the next triangle. You could use different coloured beads
for each triangle, or subtly blend from one triangle to the next.

Pass back through the third bead from the needle, pick up a bead and
go through the first bead picked up (Fig 8).

Pick up a bead. Pass the needle through bead X in the triangle you
just completed, placing the bead on top (Fig 9). Continue across to
the end, side a, in this way and pick up 5 beads. Pass back through
the third bead from the needle, pick up a bead and go through the
first bead picked up.

Pick up a bead and peyote back to the other side, using the beads
placed on top from the previous row as your base (Fig 10). Make a
turn as in Fig 4. Continue with this triangle as from Fig 5, and repeat
for the length required.

Add a magnetic clasp or make your own hidden clasp by making a loop
at one end from beads, and at the other make a 'hook' of beads by
wiring some beads into shape and stitching to the bracelet.

Experiment with:-

Colours ◆ Numbers of beads added at the turns
◆ Amount of overlap of each triangle ◆ Types and sizes of beads used

Fig 1

Fig 2

side a

Fig 3

side a

Fig 4

Fig 5

Fig 6

side a

Fig 7

side a

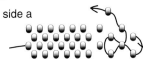

Fig 8

side a

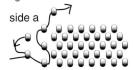

Fig 9

side a

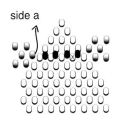

Fig 10

BRICK STITCH

Another great stitch, just as versatile as peyote, and at first glance it even looks the same - like a brick wall - though this time the right way up. But it works in a completely different way, as the beads are woven and held together through the threads and not the beads. This makes the bead fabric supple in a vertical direction.

Brick stitch is generally started off with a foundation row from which the subsequent rows can be formed, and it then produces a regular weave when Delica or seed beads are used. It is easy to see the rows of beads building up, and although tension is important, as it is with all beadwork stitches, it is not so critical as in peyote.

We have 5 lovely projects for you, again all very different (as you can see in the photo) to show you the versatility of this stitch that can be worked in so many directions - we have linear, circular and freestyle designs. And when you feel comfortable with both brick and peyote stitches, try doing a pattern that we have given you for one stitch in the other and see which you prefer . . .

The
Beadworkers
Guild

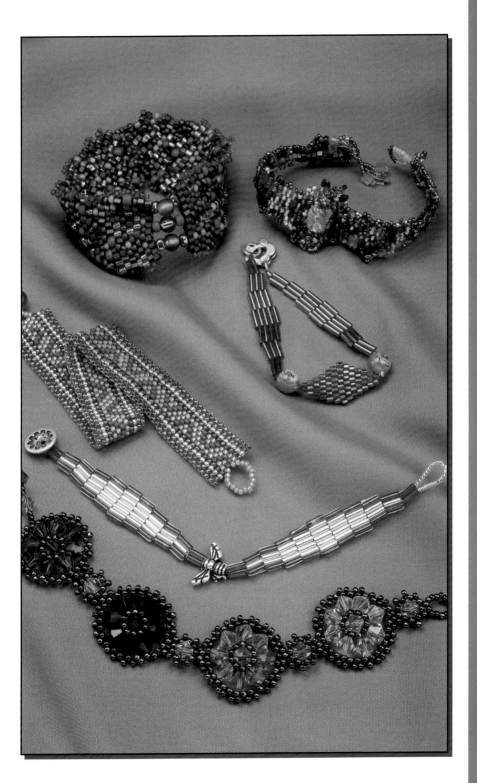

Aztec

This is a very simple and satisfying bracelet to make. But to get the suppleness in the right direction, you will have to work the whole length of the bracelet in one go, and then build up the depth. You will need to follow the chart, although the pattern is so easy you'll get the hang of it straight away!

There is a graph at the back of the book for you to create your own designs – you don't, of course, have to use the 3-Drop Brick Stitch border, but we rather like it!

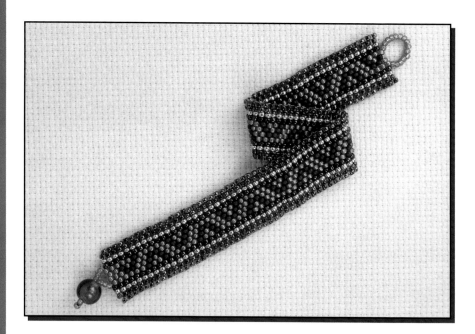

Materials
4 packets of seed beads in different colours
Fastening

Method:-
Make a foundation row 3 beads deep and 84 beads wide. Check that
this will fit around your wrist; add extra bead sets if necessary.
Work a single row of brick stitch in your main colour on the outside of
this foundation row. Then follow the chart, repeating the pattern as
required. When you have completed the pattern add a 3 bead deep
row to match the beginning, and then a further row in your main
colour.

Add a fastening of your choice on one end and a loop on the other.

Experiment with:-
Colours ◆ Design and graph other patterns in this and other stitches

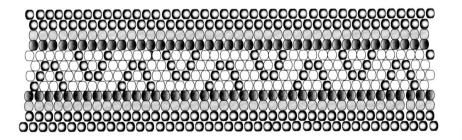

Wings

This is such a pretty design and so easy, using bugles (do be careful to check and cull them first though for nasty edges, and to make sure that they are all even. You might want to put conditioner on your thread to protect it as much as you can). We have put a feature bead in the first one – well, actually it's a silver bumblebee, and in the second variation we have used a beaded diamond shape as the centrepiece. There are so many different ways you could use this pattern – how about smaller beads which would make leaves instead of wings and overlap them? Or several smaller ones in the centre to make a daisy? Or alternating the bugles with a different bead (but with the same diameter)? Lots of ideas would look really great, but in the meantime, here's the basic pattern.

Materials

1 packet of bugle beads (plus contrast if you choose)
Feature bead
Button for clasp

Method:-

Leaving a long tail of thread, prepare a bugle foundation row of 7 beads (for the bumblebee bracelet). If you wish to use a contrast bead as in our photo then always put one on at the beginning and end of each row. Make sure that all the bugles sit tightly together – you may want to go through them twice to be sure.

On the second row and each subsequent row you will be decreasing by one bead, until there are only 2 beads left. Unthread your needle and go back to the foundation row and rethread your needle with the original thread. Work on the other side of the foundation row in the same way.

Make another piece the same and join in the centre with a feature bead. (Thread your needle, and work through to the opposite side and weave in as much as possible. If the bead is quite weighty thread through it several times.)

Add a fastening of your choice on one end and a loop on the other.

Experiment with: -

Different beads ◆ Numbers of beads
◆ Different themes and feature beads

Rosette

Doesn't this circular brick stitch bracelet look fantastic? Why make just a bracelet? How about earrings to match? Or a necklace? Or pendant? And do you know once you've got the hang of circular brick stitch you could use all sorts of beads. We've used very special swarovski crystals that give this stunning bracelet a really glamourous look.

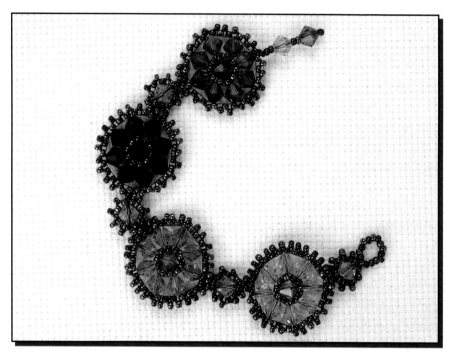

Materials
1 packet of seed beads
4 sets of 10 crystals 8mm
2 x 6mm crystals for the clasp

Method:-
Referring to the diagram on page 34, thread through a crystal in your first colour and take the thread back through again, forming a loop on the outside of the bead. Repeat this step over the top of the same thread, then twice on the opposite side. These threads will form the base to attach your first round of beads.

Pick up a seed bead, pass the needle under the base thread and back up through the seed bead just as you would on your first brick stitch row onto a foundation. Continue in this manner all the way around the centre bead, making sure that all the beads sit firmly and that there are no large gaps. When the first and last beads meet (the number will depend on the size of the beads you have used) take the thread back down the first bead then back up the last to lock them into place. End each row like this.

On the next row work crystals instead of seed beads. Our example has taken eight crystals, but yours might need more or less depending on the size you have used. Make sure that they lie flat by adjusting your tension.

On the final row pick up a seed bead, pass under the loop of thread between the crystal beads and back up through the seed bead. Then pick up 2 seed beads, pass under the loop of thread and back up through the last seed bead only. Continue in this manner all the way round. You will obviously have to put on more seed beads than there were crystals, but just keep adding as many as you need to make the rosette lie flat.

Weave the thread back through the work to the beginning tail. Tie them both together and weave back though several beads before cutting.

Make 3 more rosettes like the above.

Make 4 small rosettes: Thread up the centre large crystal as before. Work one row in seed beads to match the final row of the large rosettes. Connect all the elements together by weaving through the beads on the outer row. Finish by attaching the crystals at one end and a loop at the other.

Experiment with: -
Different beads ◆ More seed beads around the centre bead

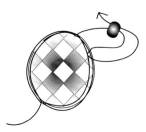

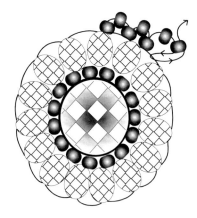

Coronet

Wow, this bracelet is rather splendid, isn't it? Don't be nervous about trying it – it is a freestyle brick stitch design, with a shaped centrepiece that reminds us of a coronet, and then the whole piece is wired to maintain its form. You can have such fun deciding what beads to use, and where to place them – and that's before you even start! Enjoy!

Materials

6 – 8 different types of beads
(Delicas, seeds, cubes, hex, triangles, etc)
1 packet of size 14 seed beads for trim
Feature bead (we used a gold foil Venetian Bead)
Small length of wire (about 25cm) gauge 24 or similar

Method:-

Make a small segment (3 or 4 cm long) of foundation row in all different sorts of beads of a fairly even size - you could use some beads 2 or even 3 drop to keep them constant (Fig 1). Turn and brick stitch the next row, varying beads, colours and textures (Fig 2).

Add enough rows for the width of the bracelet required. At one end add a foundation row extension, half the width of the central feature bead to be added. Start another piece in a similar fashion – it does not need to be the same, but you should check that it balances well. Attach the two foundation rows to the central focal bead (Fig 3 & 3A).

Make another segment to add to each side, and join on to the original section. Check length adjustment for your wrist, allowing for it to be slightly shorter – you can always add extra. Taper the width towards the centre back by reducing the size of the beads used and the number of rows worked (Fig 4).

Trim the edges with size 14 beads in a 4-bead picot.

Once the bracelet is completed, thread the wire with beads that you have already used in the bracelet – using the smallest beads that the wire will thread through. Bend the wire to the shape of your wrist, fold the ends in and firmly stitch to the bracelet.

Make a 3-stranded tassel of beads as a clasp (Fig 5), incorporating a larger bead in each tassel. Attach it to one end of the bracelet and make a loop on the other.

Experiment with:-

Colours ◆ Types and sizes of beads used
◆ Different shapes of centrepiece ◆ Width and tapering

 Fig 1

 Fig 2

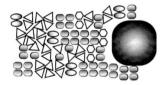

Fig 3

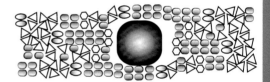

Fig 3a

 Fig 4

 Fig 5

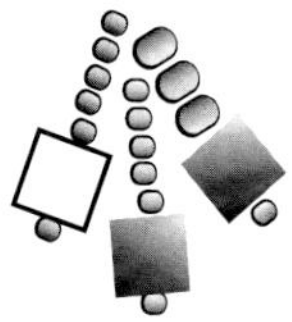

Mosaic

This is a much chunkier bracelet made with bigger beads – but of course there's nothing stopping you going into smaller, finer beads. In fact, we positively hope you will try both! The bracelet has been made in two parts with a central focal point (which could perhaps be a watch?). We have used basic brick stitch with just a little extra help at the edges to hold it firmly, and the rest is up to you – be brave, you really can use all different beads in brick stitch!

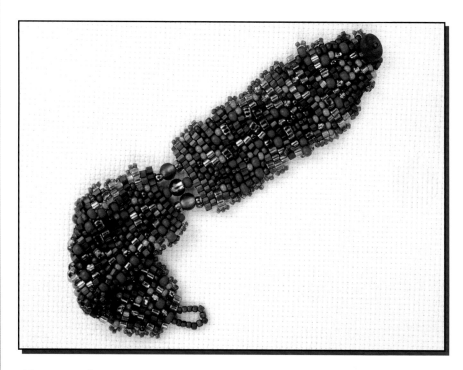

Materials
Oddments of beads incl. Double Delicas, cubes, triangles and hex beads in different sizes, seed beads size 6 and two or three colours of size 8
Toning size 14/15 for edging
3 small or 1 large feature bead for centrepiece
Feature bead for clasp

Method:-

Work a foundation row with a mid-size, even bead (we used 10 size 8 hex). On starting the next row, and for all subsequent rows to strengthen the edge, pick up two beads and square stitch them into the last 2 beads of the previous row. Then go through them again in brick stitch. (Follow the diagrams below for the thread path.)

Work all the rows randomly. If holes appear then that is part of the charm. But do keep checking the scale of the bracelet; - if you place a lot of particularly small or large beads, the width will change dramatically (which you may like!).

When you are a little less than half way around the length of your wrist stop – you can always add more later, remove your needle and start again on a second piece, trying to keep it balanced with the first.

Allowing for the clasp and the centrepiece, adjust the sizes of the two pieces and attach a clasp and a loop at either end.

Starting with fresh thread (unless you have got a very long piece left over on one side) weave in and knot around several beads towards where you first started. Join the two pieces together with the feature beads, weaving back and forth several times to add strength. Trim with a picot edge of size 14/15, and then weave in and knot your thread and cut.

Experiment with: -

Types and sizes of beads used ◆ Colours and finishes

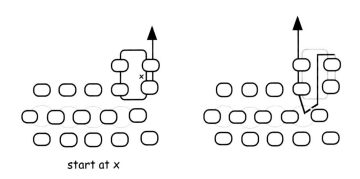

start at x

SQUARE STITCH

Imagine the foundation row of brick stitch repeated over and over, and you have the principle of square stitch. It looks at first glance like loom work – the beads sit squarely with each other. It has, of course, a great advantage over loom work – no loom! But, seriously, you can increase and decrease quite easily, and make little shapes that would be quite difficult to do on a loom. It also provides a wonderful base to embellish with both square and other stitches.

Square stitch does however, use a lot of thread, and it does show, so use a toning colour. You will also be passing through your beads quite a few times, so a finer needle and thread than you usually need would be a sensible precaution. (B thread and 13 needle).

We have included some lovely patterns that work very well in square stitch, but we have not included any more freestyle designs as we think you will have got the idea by now about experimenting.
But, just as we have for the other stitches, we have included graph paper at the back of the book so that you can chart up your own designs, or transfer them from other mediums, such as knitting or cross stitch . . .

The
Beadworkers
Guild

Stripes & Diamonds Cuffs

We've chosen two lovely designs, both following the same technique, which can be made in square stitch. You just need to follow the relevant chart.

You can make your cuff as long as you want to by following the repeats (you could of course make it into a choker and add a fringe!). As with the other stitches, there is a graph at the back of the book for you to make your own designs, or you could adapt from a cross-stitch, needlepoint or knitting pattern!

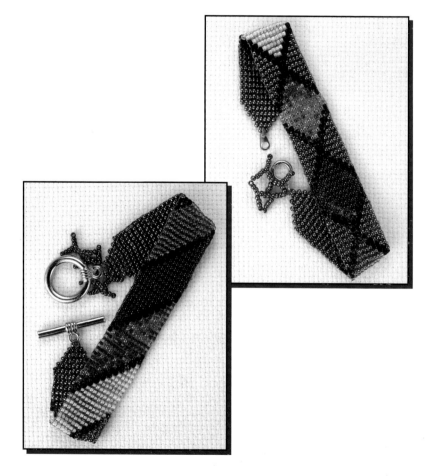

Materials (For either pattern)
6 packets of seed beads in different colours
Clasp

Method:-
Thread on 12 beads in your main colour. Using the square stitch instructions follow the graph provided.

When you have finished the pattern, decrease on each of the following rows by one bead on either side, until there are two beads left. Unthread your needle and repeat this on the other end. Check the size on your wrist, allowing for the clasp. If it is too long then remove rows equally. If it is too short then add rows of two beads equally. For a bit of fun add some strands of beads and attach to one end of the bracelet. Attach a clasp.

Experiment with:-
Patterns ◆ Colours

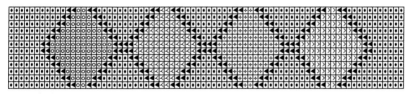

Diamonds

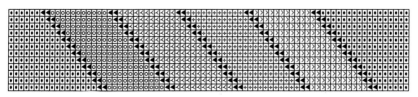

Stripes

Tiles

We have two different versions of this pattern for you, the same design in different sizes – they both look great, try them! You could also try using different sized beads, possibly in the same bracelet? The pattern you will be following is the smaller bronze Tiles.

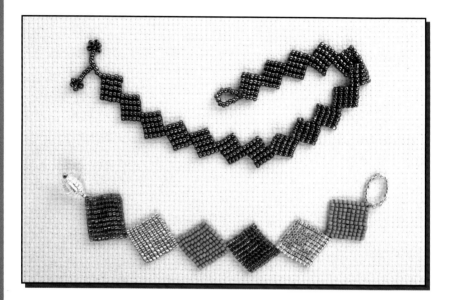

Materials
1 packet of seed beads (or Delica Beads)

Method:-
Thread on 5 beads. Following the square stitch instructions, work 3 rows. At the end of the last row, pick up a further 5 beads. *Keeping the tension taut, work square stitch over all 10 beads (see Fig 1).

Pass the needle back through all the lower 'double' row except Bead D; then go up through the bead on the edge of the top row (Bead E) and start the next square stitch row on top of this bead (see Fig 2).

Square stitch across the next 4 beads, turn and work one more row. Pick up a further 5 beads and repeat from* until you have the length you require.

Make a beaded toggle at one end and a loop top fit at the other.

Experiment with:-
Bead sizes ◆ Numbers of beads used
◆ Embellishments (e.g. squares on squares)

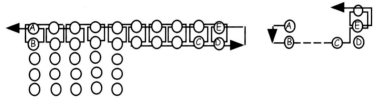

Fig 1   Fig 2

Union Jack

This is 'groovy baby'! If you've got a teenage friend this is just the one for her! Why not make this for one wrist and the Star Spangled Bracelet (peyote stitch) for the other. To do this design is straightforward, just follow the pattern. You could of course try different colours, or change the pattern, or make your own with the graph paper at the back of the book!

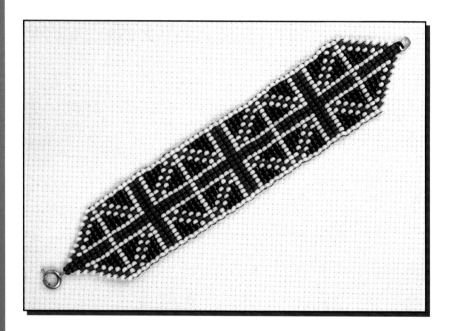

Materials

1 packet each red, white and blue Delica beads
Clasp

Method:-

Thread on 18 beads and follow the chart. When the pattern has been repeated 3 times decrease on each row by one bead either side, continuing to follow the pattern, until there are two beads left. Unthread your needle and repeat this on the other end. Check the size on your wrist, allowing for the clasp. If it is too long then remove rows equally. If it is too short then add rows of two beads equally. Attach the clasp.

Experiment with:-

Colours ◆ Graphing other designs in this stitch or other stitches

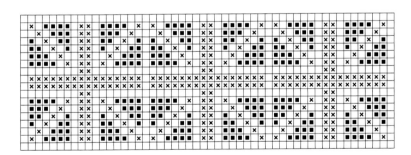

HERRINGBONE WEAVE

What a lovely stitch this is, quick and easy, and so elegant. It makes a beautiful, supple fabric, with the most interesting pattern of beads. Indeed the stitch structure is so attractive that it really doesn't need any fancy designs or embellishments on it. It seems to look best in beads that have a more tubular or square shape, such as Delicas or hex beads – they really accentuate the chevron design.

The stitch is a little bit difficult to get the hang of but, as in Peyote, keep going, and you can always pull the first few rows off once you are in the swing of it. (But, unlike peyote, you can't go back and stitch more on in the opposite direction – this is very much a one-way stitch, so practise first.)

We have chosen some designs for you in bold blocks of colour that show off the stitch to perfection, and if you really need to do something more with this stitch, try adding extra beads infilled between the rows to create a textured effect . . .

The
Beadworkers
Guild

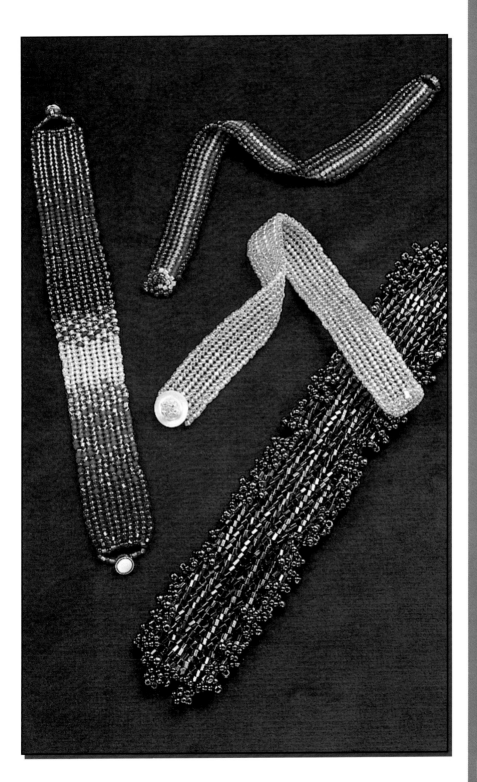

Patches & Pinstripes

Our patches are pretty pastels, but you could have them bold and brassy – herringbone weave is so interesting in itself that large blocks of any colour work well!

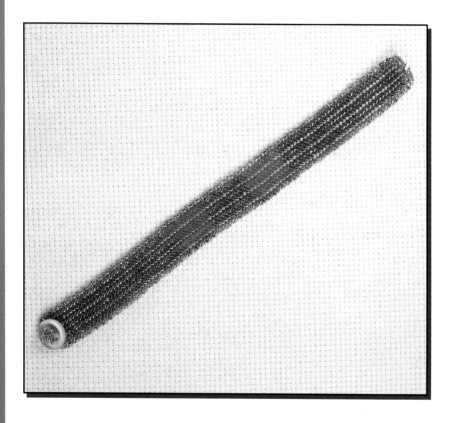

Materials
1 packet each of pink and green Delicas
Pearly button

Method:-
Make the foundation and work Rows 1 & 2 exactly as in the
herringbone weave instructions. Use pink (P) as the light beads and
green (G) as the dark.

1st pink patch Row A: use 2G for the edge, and then pick up 2P, 2P,
and 2P. Repeat Row A until this patch is as long as you want it to be
(ours is 30 rows).

1st green patch Row B: Pick up 1G and 1P for the edge, and then pick
up 2P, 2P, and 2P. Row C: Use 2P for the edge, and then pick up 2G,
2G, and 2G. Repeat Row C until this patch is as long as you want it to
be (ours is 11 rows).

2nd pink patch Row D: Pick up 1P and 1G for the edge, and then pick
up 2P, 2P, and 2P. Work as many of Row A as you need to match the
1st green patch.

2nd green patch – work as for the 1st green patch.

3rd pink patch – work 1 Row D and as many of Row A as you need to
match the 1st pink patch.

Green stripe: use 2G on the edge; 2G, 2G, and 2G. * Pink stripe: use
1G and 1P on the edge; 2P, 2P, and2P. Green stripe: use 1P and 1G on
the edge; and 2G, 2G, and 2G. Repeat from * once. Work one more
pink row. Pick up 1P and put the needle back through all the beads of
the last row and fasten off.

Stitch a decorated button on one end of the bracelet. Make a loop of
beads at the other end to fit.

Experiment with:-
Different colours and sizes of beads ◆ Different edgings

Rainbow

This slender rainbow arches over your wrist beautifully. Working in stripes like this is a really good way to become familiar with herringbone weave. If you want to make the bracelet wider, use two beads instead of one - then, if you like, you can use all 7 colours of the rainbow!

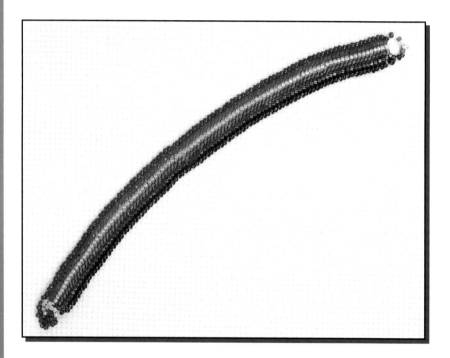

Materials

1 packet each of seed beads or Delicas in red (R), orange (O), yellow (Y), green (G), blue (B) and purple (P).

Method:-

Following the basic herringbone weave instructions, make the foundation with 13 beads using the following colours for step 1: 2P, 2B, 2G, 2Y, 2O and 3R. For step 3 of the foundation, pick up in this order: 1O & 1Y and 1G & 1B.

In Row 1, pick up 2P, then 1B & 1G then 1Y & 1O.
In Row 2, pick up 2R, then 1O & 1Y then 1G & 1B.

Repeat rows 1 and 2 until you have the length you require.

Make a little button of spiralling peyote in the primary colours, as we have done (see the basic techniques chapter), or use a button from your collection, to stitch on to one end of the bracelet. Make a loop of beads to fit at the other end.

Experiment with:-

Different colours and sizes of beads ◆ Wider stripes

Spectrum

Wear a colour wheel on your wrist! The bands of colour in this bracelet shade from hot red through to sparkling purple. In some blocks we have used two shades or two different finishes for extra depth of colour, but you can keep it simple if you prefer. Depending on the size of your beads and the size of your wrist, you may need to adjust the number of rows you have in each block, so instructions for doing that are given as well.

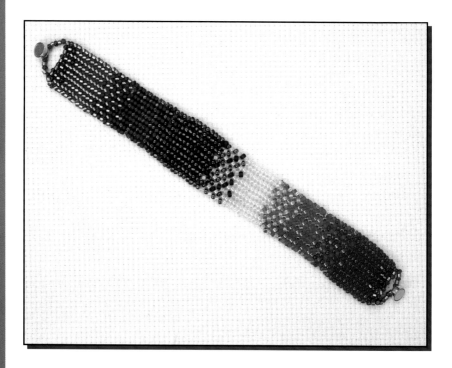

Materials

1 packet each of seed beads or Delicas in red, frosted and shiny orange, yellow, two shades of green, frosted and shiny blue and purple.
Fastening

Method:-

Following the basic herringbone weave instructions start at A on the chart and make the foundation with 21 alternating red and purple beads, starting and ending with purple. Work in herringbone weave until you reach point B. Measure the length you have so far, multiply by 6 and add enough to accommodate the clasp. If that would make the bracelet too short (or long) for your wrist, decide how many extra (or fewer) rows you will need for the whole bracelet and divide by six to give you the number of rows you will need for each block of colour. Undo the last four rows and work the required extra rows in plain red (or undo the excess rows of plain red). Continue to follow the chart, remembering to adjust the number of rows in each block as necessary. If you are using two shades or finishes in one colour, pick them up randomly as you go along.

Needle through the last row to firm it and attach a loop of beads with a clasp in the centre. Repeat at the other end of the bracelet.

Experiment with:-

Different colours and sizes of beads ◆ Adding odd beads between the rows to create a textured effect

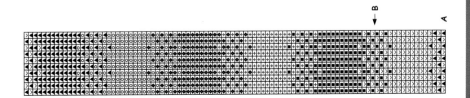

Copper Ruffles

The light glinting off the facets of these copper coloured hex beads really show up beautifully the pattern of slanting pairs of beads which gives herringbone weave its name. We have added a sumptuous ruffled edging as a counterpoint.

Materials

2 packets copper hex beads size 11/12, and 1 each of copper seed beads in size 11/12 and 8

Method:-

Following the basic herringbone weave instructions, start the foundation with 21 hex beads and continue until the bracelet is as long as required. Make two beaded beads at one end, and two loops of beads at the other.

For the ruffle, join in a new thread and bring the needle out at the top of the bead on one edge of the last row worked (bead A in the diagram). Pick up two seed beads, put the needle into the bottom of bead A and through the same two seed beads again. * Pick up another two seed beads and put the needle into the bottom of the next bead below on the edge of the bracelet and through the same two seed beads again. Repeat from * all the way down this edge of the bracelet. Work back along the edge picking up one or two beads and going through every seed bead. Vary the size of beads you pick up as much as you can and pull the work up tight. Work the other side of the bracelet to match.

Experiment with:-

Different colours and finishes ◆ Different bead shapes
◆ Other edgings

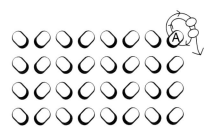

RIGHT ANGLE WEAVE

Now here's a stitch that has everything – it can work flat, circular, tubular, and 3D; it can increase and decrease beautifully; it can cover all manner of unusually shaped objects, and it has a fluidity and drape in all directions that would make cloth envious! So what's the catch? Well, for some people none at all. For others a little extra concentration might be needed in the beginning. Think figures of eight, and you'll be there. The beads sit at right angles to one another placed by a thread path that turns clockwise and anti-clockwise, but never straight.

You can have 4 beads making up each little group, or you can have 24 - it's not the number that counts but the way the thread travels.

We have devised some really easy patterns for you to help you gat used to this unique stitch, and we defy you not to be hooked . . .

The
Beadworkers
Guild

Gala & Lattice

Two glamourous bracelets for eveningwear, and simple to do! These bracelets are a terrific introduction to right angle weave, both of them being just two rows. We have used crystals so that you can understand the thread path of the stitch clearly. In Lattice, the green and white one in the picture, we have opened out the weave by adding in seed beads to create an open, lacy effect.

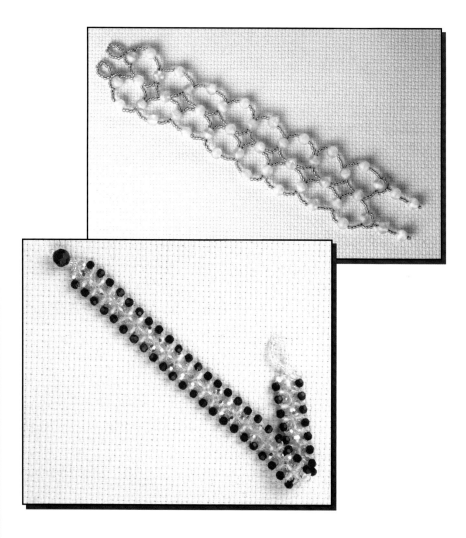

Materials

Gala

70 6mm crystals in red
175 6mm crystals in clear
1 8mm crystal for clasp
A few seed beads for loop of clasp

Lattice

50 6mm round beads
1 packet seed beads

Method:-

Work both bracelets by following the right angle weave instructions closely. The sequences of beads to pick up are described below

Gala

Row 1:   Step 1; Pick up 1 red crystal and 3 clear crystals
            Step 2; 2 clear and 1 red
            Step 3; 1 red and 2 clear
Row 2:   turn as described in the right angle weave
            instructions and pick up as follows
            Step 4; 1 clear 1 red and 1 clear

Lattice   Work 2 rows of right angle weave. Each circle in
            the diagrams represents 1 6mm bead. 4 seed
            beads are picked up in between each 6mm bead so
            start by picking up 1 6mm bead & 4 seed beads
            four times. The weave is thus expanded, but the
            thread path remains exactly as in the basic
            instructions.

Finish with a bead toggle and loop for the fastening (double for Lattice so that the bracelet will lay flat on your wrist).

Experiment with:-

Different combinations and types of beads

Cable

This is a very basic right-angle weave with embellishments - you can see from the photo some of the possibilities, it's so fun and tactile, and really very easy and quick to do!

Materials

2 packets of different coloured seed beads

Clasp of your choice

Use a finer needle than usual for this project, as you will be passing through the beads quite a few times

Method:-

Pick up 2 Main (M), 1 Contrast (C), 1M 1C 2M 1C 1M and 1C and tie in a knot. Pass through the 2M 1C 1M 1C and 2M. *Add 1C 1M 1C 2M 1C 1M and 1C, and pass through the last 2M already threaded but in the opposite direction. Pass through 1C 1M 1C 2M and repeat from *. Continue until the bracelet is the desired length. Attach your button clasp (or whatever you have chosen to use) now. This first section is the foundation upon which the pattern can be built. And from here you can make all sorts of patterns. We will do a basic crossover.

Bring your needle out of one side or the other of the end 2M. Add 1M 1C and 1M and pass the needle diagonally through the opposite corner M bead, and then through the 2nd M. Add 1M 1C and 1M and repeat down to the bottom of the bracelet, always following in the same direction. Attach the loop for your clasp now.

Now go back up the bracelet by exiting from the M bead, add 1M, pass through the C bead, add 1M and pass the needle diagonally through the opposite corner M bead. Pass the needle through the 2nd M and continue up the bracelet until the end.

Experiment with:-

Leaving some circles empty ◆ Changing the centre bead(s)
◆ Making several and joining them together ◆ Work on both sides

Zip

The photograph can only hint at the slinky, sensuous feel of this bracelet. It drapes so gracefully, that we feel sure you will want to make a necklace to match! Go for sophisticated golds and silvers for a classic look or vibrant, tropical colours for stunning effect. We cannot pretend that right angle weave worked in seed beads is the easiest beading you will ever learn, but the results are well worth the effort, and once you've cracked it you'll love it. We have kept the design simple and the central stripe is there especially to assist you in 'zipping' up right angle weave!

Materials

1 packet each of blue (M) and silver (C) seed beads
Fastening

Method:-

Following the right angle weave instructions, work the first row by picking up 4M, 3M, 2M & 1C 3M, 3M. For the second row pick up 3M, 1M & 1C, 2C, 2M, 2M. Repeat the second row until the bracelet is the required length.

Work one row entirely in M. * Next row; needle through so that you exit from the bottom of the next 'square'. Work the row picking up 3M, 2M, and 2M. **Needle back round the last 'square' made and through the two bottom beads of the other two squares in the last row. Attach the fastening to the three bottom beads of the last row.

Work the other end of the bracelet to match.

Experiment with:-

Different sizes and colours of beads ◆ Different numbers of beads in each 'square' ◆ Filling each 'square'

DAISY BRAIDS

Don't dismiss the humble daisy braid - you really don't have to make little flowers (but, of course, you can if you want to). You can make endless variations with just a six-bead daisy by varying the colour placements, and then of course there are eight-bead daisies (which look nothing like daisies) and double daisy braids!

We have included just three different variations for you, and some patterns for you to devise your own – photocopy them and have fun with your colouring pencils! And when you've made more bracelets than your wrist can carry, you'll find umpteen cushions and jumpers just crying out for braided edges . . .

The
Beadworkers
Guild

Daisy Braids

There are lots of different ways to make daisy braids, and lots of variations you can do. Look at the diagrams to get started and then try using different numbers of beads and/or different colour sequences. You can even add several braids together for a really interesting effect.

Materials
2 packets of different coloured seed beads

Method:-
Basic 6-bead daisy:
Pick up 6 beads, tie in a circle and pass through the 1st bead again. Pick up 1 contrast bead and pass through bead no 4. *Pick up 4 beads and pass through bead no 5. Pick up 1 contrast bead and pass through bead no 9. Repeat from *. See the diagrams for variations.

Variation 4:
This double braid is worked the entire length as above and then a second row is added to the side. Remember that you will already have one side bead in place, so you will pick up 1 less bead each time than on the basic row.

Basic 8-bead daisy:

This is constructed in a slightly different way: instead of making the outside ring first and then adding the inside bead, you start off with half the outside ring, then add the middle, and then the second half of the outside ring, as in the diagram.

Experiment with:-
Colours ◆ Patterns ◆ Types and sizes of beads used

Basic 6-Bead Daisy

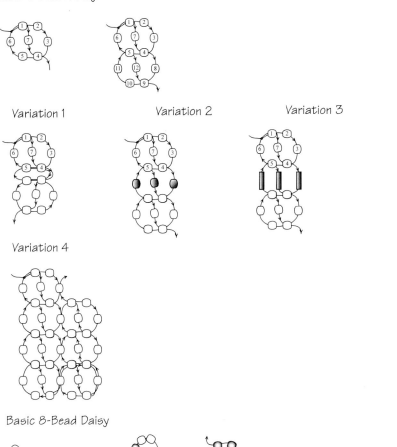

Variation 1

Variation 2

Variation 3

Variation 4

Basic 8-Bead Daisy

Step 1   Step 2   Step 3   Step 4

Repeat steps 3 and 4
for the length desired

TUBULAR STITCHES

Here we have tubular versions of some of the stitches in the first part of the book. They are all easy to do, but we recommend that you gain confidence in the particular stitch before trying it in the round.

The tubular herringbone starts off in a slightly different way from the flat version – try both and make up your own mind up.

The white and black/gold bracelets in the top right-hand of the photo opposite are tubular or 3D right angle weave – they are the Cable Bracelet turned over and worked on both sides. Very easy and very effective.

When you have tried these patterns you could devise tubular versions of your own for all the stitches: you could keep them plain as very superior cords, you could add a special focal bead, or if you really feel a beady moment coming on then embellish them to your hearts content . . .

The
Beadworkers
Guild

Snakes — *(Tubular Herringbone)*

This stitch is surprising easy to do and very quick to make up. We have started the first couple of rows slightly differently to the flat version – you can do either but we think this foundation for brick stitch beginning is a little easier to hold, and easier to start off in the round. It also helps to have a firm ending to the rope for attaching the clasp. In this version we have added a little bit of extra interest by including some additional infill beads – they are not necessary to make the herringbone stitch but create an added texture.

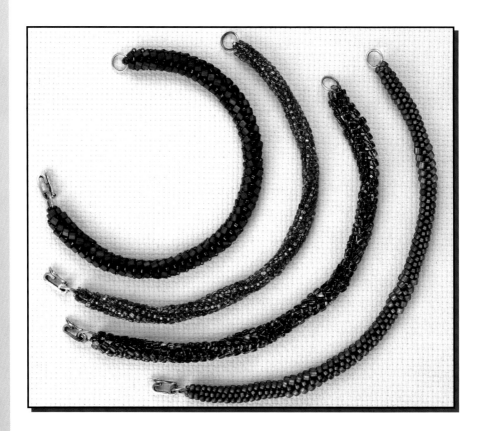

Materials

1 Packet size 8 hex bead and 1 Packet Delicas in contrast colour
Fastening

Method:-

Prepare a brick stitch foundation 2 beads high, 4 beads wide and tie
in a knot to form a circle. Pass through again to strengthen.
Thread on 1 hex (H), 1 Delica (D) and 1H and pass the needle back
down the next bead in the stack. Pass the needle up through the next
bead in the stack (Fig 1), thread on 1H 1D and 1H and pass the needle
down through the remaining bead in the stack.

Working in the same direction pass up through the original bead in the
sequence, and through the one above just placed on (Fig 2), add 1H 1D
and 1H and pass <u>down</u> into the next bead in the stack. Continue in
this fashion until the rope is the desired length. Add a fastening of
your choice on one end and a loop on the other.

Experiment with:-

Different shapes and sizes of beads ◆ Different infill beads in both
the front and the side ◆ Changing bead sizes within the same piece

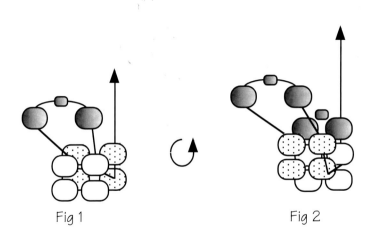

Fig 1   Fig 2

Tyres – *(Tubular Netting)*

These bracelets are lovely to make and lovely to wear – not least because you don't need a clasp – just roll them on! We give you the basic instructions, and after that it's up to you: how about an inner and an outer coil (like the one in the photo)? How about different beads on one of the coils? How about using nylon fishing line instead of Nymo thread to give the bracelet even more body and stretch? All those choices!

Materials
1 packet seed beads and 1 packet contrasting seed beads

Method:-
Thread on 15 beads in the sequence 1 Contrast Bead (C) 2 Main Beads (M). Bring the needle round and pass it through the first bead to form a circle (Fig 1). Keep your work flat on the table to start with.

Pick up 2M 1C 2M and pass the needle through Bead 3.
Pick up 2M 1C and 2M and pass the needle through Bead 5.
Pick up 2M 1C and 2M and pass the needle through Bead 6 (Fig 2).

Try to pull the beads tight at this stage and then continue adding groups in the same manner and passing the needle through every 2nd C. If you find it difficult to see where to go at first, then just loosen the thread again and work flat on the table a little longer. Remember that, once the pattern is established, you can make the tube as long as you like and then take off the first few beads anyway, so don't worry about them.

When the bracelet is the desired length you can 'seam' the two ends of the tube together. Aim for an invisible join. Tie the beginning and end threads together, and weave both in for a few stitches before cutting.

Experiment with:-
Using different shapes and sizes of beads ◆ Using different combinations of Main bead ◆ Creating a tube within a tube
◆ Embellish with loops of beads

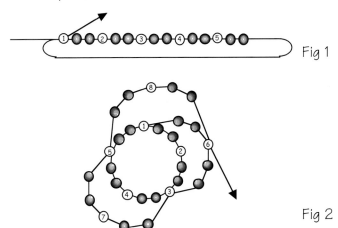

Fig 1

Fig 2

Bindweed & Seaweed Charm Bracelets
– (Tubular Peyote Stitch)

Don't these look pretty? But really there's nothing to it – a peyote
tube embellished with whatever takes your fancy – we've gone for two
different takes around the same theme; a charm bracelet with dangly
bits. (You can see the seaweed version in the photo at the beginning
of the chapter) You wind the 'weed' around the rope foundation and
add bits and pieces. In the centre of each bracelet we've made a
focal point of extra texture where the 'weed' is particularly dense to
give added interest both visually and allegorically. You can have great
fun working out your own theme, and collecting the bits and pieces to
put on your bracelet.

Materials

1 packet seed beads
1 or 2 packets of toning transparent size 14/15 seed beads
Various feature beads, charms, shells, gemstone chips etc (approx 20 – 30 depending on size)
Feature or beaded bead for clasp

Method:-

Make a 7-bead peyote tube – thread on 7 seed beads and tie into a loop. Work in the same manner as for flat peyote. (You will find that by starting with an uneven number of beads your work will spiral upwards. If you use an even number of beads you will have to step up at the end of each row.) You may find it easier to start off your tube if you put a small cocktail or kebab stick inside it to give you something to work around. When your rope is the required length it is time to start adding the 'weed'. Pick up 5 – 9 size 14/15 seed beads and sew them onto the tube following a downwards spiral. Go all the way down the rope in this fashion, varying the number of beads added, including feature beads where you think, and branched fringing as the mood takes you. When you have finished, turn around and go back again to halfway, this time adding little peyote shapes and more embellishments. (The reason for doing this twice is to get the positioning correct. On the initial run you can concentrate on positioning the 'weed' and on the second run in thickening and embellishing.) At the halfway point add considerably more fringing, by making a 5-bead fringe from every bead in the tube, to a width of about 5 beads. If you have some small feature beads or gemstone chips, etc, include them in this cluster. When you think that the cluster looks thick enough, continue adding to the 'weed'. When you are satisfied with the overall balance of the bracelet, add a feature or beaded bead on one end, and a loop on the other.

Experiment with:-

Different types of tube base made with different stitches and varying widths ◆ Different embellishments – bead your own flowers, leaves, butterflies etc ◆ Cover the whole rope with tactile fringing

BEADED BEADS

These beaded beads are very satisfying to make, and surprisingly easy. You make each bead separately and then string them together in endless permutations.

You can see from the photo that we have included plain tubes that we have not embellished (the gold ones at the top), and various bought beads – carved turquoise and some flower beads. We just love all the different textures, and you too can have a great time gathering your different elements together before you start work.

The beaded beads we have chosen are simplicity itself, but oh, so tactile! You could of course, come up with umpteen variations now that you know so many stitches, and they would all be quite stunning.

Start with these, and see what we mean . . .

The
Beadworkers
Guild

Bubbles

These look fun don't they? They are really easy (you can make mistakes here, no one will ever know), and they are very satisfying to make. Basically you will be making various beaded beads and then stringing them together. So think carefully about your colour/tonal palette, and the overall look you want to create before you start. You could make your bracelet with all your beaded beads the same, or you could make each one different, or you could, as we have, choose a central bead and make each side symmetrical.

Materials
1 packet silver-lined Delica beads
1 packet dark frosted seed beads size 8
2 different packets seed beads size 14/15
1 or 2 beads with largish central hole to bead around (optional)
2 - 6 feature beads (optional)
A few seed beads size 6 for spacing
Soft-flex wire and crimps or heavy thread for stringing
Fastening

Method: -
To make the base for these beads you could use either tubular brick or peyote stitch, whichever you feel most comfortable with (or make flat rectangles and seam the edges into a tube). For a peyote tube thread on 7 or 8 Delica beads and tie into a loop. For a brickstitch tube work a foundation row of 7 or 8 beads. Work in the same manner as for flat peyote/flat brick stitch. It is important that you use Delica, or similar large-holed beads because you will be passing thread through them many times. Make your tube about 6mm long. You may find it easier to work your tube on a small cocktail or kebab stick to give you something to work around, it will also help you to find the opening later. Make approximately 9 of these tube bases and then embellish them.

When you have covered them to your satisfaction, arrange them in a pleasing sequence. Use size 6 beads to act as buffers between each beaded bead so that they may be seen clearly. Add any feature beads you may wish to use, and check for length. String them onto either soft-flex wire (which you crimp to fasten) or heavy thread, and attach a fastening.

Experiment with:-

Varying colours and tones of beads ◆ Different combinations of beaded beads ◆ Embellishing beads with freeform peyote or brick stitch ◆ Covering beads with peyote, brick stitch, right-angle weave, etc

RUFFLES

These are very quick and effective: just add a 5-bead netting edge to either side of the tube, as deep as you would like.

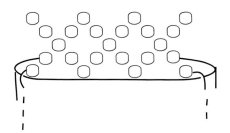
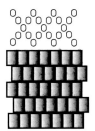

SPIKEYS

Starting on the top of the tube, come out of a Delica and, working your way around and down, add 1 size 8 bead and 1 size 14. Pass the needle back down through the size 8 bead and backstitch it through the other side of the Delica you came out of. Cover the entire bead in this fashion. If it looks a little sparse, just go in and add some more, but try to make sure they all sit well together. You can vary the depth of the Spikeys by adding a size 11 bead between the 8 and the 14.

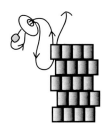

STALKIES

Starting on the top of the tube, come out of a Delica and, working your way around and down, add a fringe of 4 Delicas and 1 size 14. Pass the needle back down through the Delicas and backstitch through the other side of the Delica you came out of. Cover the entire bead in this fashion. If it looks sparse, start all the way over again – you could change your bead colour as well if you choose, or make the second set slightly longer or shorter.

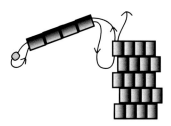

FLUFFIES

Starting on the top of the tube, come out of a Delica and, working your way around and down, add a loop of 3 size 14s. Backstitch through the other side of the Delica you came out of. Cover the entire bead in this fashion. If it looks sparse, start all the way over again, maybe this time changing the bead colour slightly. You could vary the appearance of this Fluffy by making one slightly bigger – use a 5-bead loop.

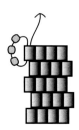

WRAPPED BEADS

Using a large plastic or wooden bead (approx 10 mm) as a base, pass your thread through the hole and tie tightly. Add as many size 14 beads as are needed to cover the outside of the large bead and pass through. Pass your needle through the first 1 (or 2) beads of the previous row (how many you go through will depend on the curvature of the large bead) add on more size 14 beads less 2 (or 4) and pass through the last 1 (or 2) beads of that same previous row. Push this wedge shape to one side and continue adding beads in the same fashion until the large bead is covered. . If you are using a particularly awkwardly shaped bead you may want to add some knots at the top or bottom of the large bead, to hold the seed beads in place. Then add a size 6 bead to either end to cover any mistakes; making sure that it is central. Tie off the thread ends and bury.

SPIRALS

We loved doing these so much we couldn't stop! The permutations are endless: and the different styles that can be achieved are also endless: elegant, chunky or dainty, try them all.

In the photo opposite the four central bracelets and the blue and the yellow/green are all variations of the Dutch Spiral, which, as you can see, changes it's character for every different set of beads used. The rest are the Spiral Staircase, which is a thin and elegant design.

Of course, you don't have to even stick to the same pattern throughout - why not add some peyote stitch for example into one of the axis of the Dutch Spiral, or a different size of beads in a centre section?

And if you want to make necklaces as well, just keep going . . .

The
Beadworkers
Guild

Spiral Staircase

This is such an elegant spiral rope, and so easy to do. It is a particularly strong stitch, so makes a good strap for a bag. All you have to imagine is that you are adding beads and going up a staircase, one step at a time. You can also have great fun varying the size and number of beads used and the colours – why stick at one shade throughout the rope, how about varying the tones?

Materials
1 packet dark seed beads for the inside spiral core
1 packet light seed beads for the outside of the spiral
Fastening

Method:-
Pick up 4 dark seed beads (colour A) and 3 light seed beads (Colour B).
Tie the beads into a circle. Pass the needle through the 4A. Pick up
1A and 3B* and let the beads drop down to the work (Fig 1). Pass the
needle up through the last 3A and the A just added (Fig 2). Pull the
thread up firmly.

Position the outside beads you just added until they sit right next to
the three previously placed outside beads. Pick up 1A and 3B and
repeat the process from * until you have the length you wish.
(It will take 8 or 9 repetitions of the basic stitch before a spiral
begins to appear.)

Attach a fastening of your choice to one end, and a loop to the other.

Experiment with:-
Types, colours and numbers of beads

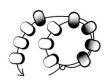

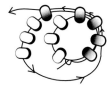

Fig 1   Fig 2

Dutch Spiral

If you are completely new to this sort of beading start with the pattern that we have explained to you. It is really easy to work in bugles, and once you have worked the first few rows, you can see the spiral starting to happen and you'll be well away. If you want a more elegant look, use all the same size beads for your project, and if you want a more textural piece use all different sized beads (not necessarily one of each, you can use any multiples you like). All you have to remember is that you are working in sets of threes (a triangular concept), and that it is easier for you if you make each of the 3 central axis beads bigger than the sets of 3 transitional beads. Here are some examples:

Also note that the bigger the size differences the more the pattern will undulate.

Materials
1 packet each of bugle and seed (or similar) beads
Fastening

Method:-
You may like to condition your thread for those bugle beads, and do check them carefully, this design is particularly prone to broken threads because of the angle that the beads are placed.
Take as long a piece of thread as you can manage, leaving a long tail that will be used later to make the pyramid terminal.

Referring to the diagrams overleaf, pick up 1 Bugle (B), 1 Seed bead (S), 1B 1S 1B 1S. Pass the thread through all the 6 beads and knot, and then through the first B and S again.

Pick up 1S 1B and pass the needle through the next S. Gently pull tight. Continue to pick up 1S 1B and pass the needle through the next S, and after a few rows you will see the spiral forming. Keep the tension of the work fairly tight and check your work regularly. When you have reached the desired length sew through the last row again to strengthen. (If you get confused about which bead to add, remember that whichever axis bead you have gone through – which in this example will be a seed bead – thread on another of the same.)

To make the pyramid terminals pick up enough S to cover the B + S and pass the needle back through the S and B so that the new S's sit on top. Pass through the S's again and move on to the next B and S. Repeat all the way round. For the next row pick up 1 less S than in the previous row and pass the needle back through the first set of S's so that the new set sit on top of the first set. Continue the process forming the pyramid until you have 3 single S's on top. Unthread your needle and repeat this procedure for the other end of the bracelet. Allowing for your clasp, check your length. If it is too long then remove rows equally. If it is too short then add further rows equally. Attach your clasp.

Experiment with:-
Different beads for both axis and transition groups ◆ Different numbers of beads in any of the sections ◆ Increasing and decreasing the numbers of beads in one of the transition groups ◆ Including a peyote stitch section in one of the axis

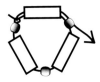

Pyramid Terminals

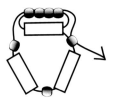

BASIC TECHNIQUES

In this section we cover basic beadworking techniques which will help you make the bracelets in this book. We hope you will also use it as a general reference to turn to when your memory needs to be jogged on a "how to". We are not giving you rules, only guidance, and in some cases have suggested more than one way of tackling a particular task. This is because some methods will suit a particular stitch or project better than others; and you might simply feel personally more comfortable with one way of, say, fastening in a new thread, than the others. Many of you will already have developed your own personal style and beadworking habits; those who haven't, probably soon will! That's fine. Whatever works for you is the right way.

GETTING STARTED

A stop bead can be really useful when picking up the first group of beads because it does just what it says - stops them falling off again! You don't have to use one, of course. But for some stitches which are difficult to control in the early stages, like peyote or herringbone weave, it is particularly helpful. For others, e.g. a brick stitch foundation, you probably won't bother.

String a bead which is obviously different in colour from the beads for your design (saves confusion!) and loop through it again once or twice. Once the work is established, just pull the stop bead off.

Whether or not you use a stop bead, always leave a long tail of thread for fastening off/making clasps later.

JOINING IN A NEW THREAD
AND FASTENING OFF THE OLD

1. Weave the new thread through the beadwork so that it exits from the same bead as the old thread. If the stitch you are using is a loose style, e.g. a daisy braid, then a few knots on to the working thread along the way would be a good idea. A good way to do this is to put the needle underneath the thread in between two beads and draw it down into a small loop; go through the loop once or twice and pull slowly so that the loop is drawn down to nestle in the beadwork. If the stitch is one of the close fitting types, e.g. peyote, make sure you turn a few circles as you weave into position and you shouldn't need to knot. Carry on working with the new thread before weaving the old thread into the new beadwork (this avoids the problem of "packed" beads in the work before the join).

2. Another approach is to knot the old and new threads together and then weave the ends into the beadwork as described above. A good knot for this purpose is a square knot (right over left, left over right), but be very careful to manoeuvre the knot into exactly the right place before you tighten it - guiding it with a needle or pair of tweezers in the centre of the knot will help.

BEADED "TOGGLE" AND LOOP FASTENINGS

It is very important to make the toggle first so that you can work the loop to fit it.

The Toggle

1. This is like making a fringe (not used in any of the bracelets - but why not if you fancy it?). Thread a few seed beads for a stem, pick up a large bead and one seed bead, turn and go back down the large bead and stem beads. The seed bead at the end acts as an anchor. You can of course use a combination of different sized beads in the stem if you wish.

2. Use a beaded bead at the end of a stem of beads and it will match your bracelet to perfection. Two types of beaded bead are described in this chapter.

The Loop

The important thing here is the fit. Thread on a guestimate of beads, put the needle back down through the first bead (eye first!) and, holding the thread very tightly, test the loop over the toggle. The number of beads in the loop should be adjusted so that it just fits - too loose, and bracelet is lost; too tight and you can't do it up (or break the loop in the attempt!). When satisfied, fasten the thread off securely into the beadwork.

There are some new beading elastics on the market which will go through seed beads and can be used for the loops, making measuring less crucial and the fastening potentially more secure. But they require crimps to fix in place, or a double knot which can't be easily buried into the beadwork, both of which can be unsightly and/or uncomfortable.

THICK THREAD INTO A SMALL BEAD

Sometimes, you need to get a thicker thread (or elastic) through a seed bead than your beading needle can accommodate. Try using a pearl threading needle, which is fine twisted wire with a loop for an eye which flattens as it goes through the bead, or make one of your own: thread a couple of inches of Nymo into a beading needle, tie into a loop and thread your heavier thread through the loop.

BEADED BEADS

Bobbly Bead

If you are making a bobbly bead for the end of a toggle, it is usually easiest to make the bead first, thread on a few beads for the stem and then stitch into the bracelet.

Pick up 3 beads and tie into a ring, leaving an end long enough to neaten off later. Pick up one bead and put the needle through the centre of the ring - the bead is caught on one side. Pick up another bead and go back again through the centre. Continue adding beads in the same way - always going through gaps not beads

- until the bead is the size you want. If you want to even up the shape (though part of its charm is the bobbly texture) put the needle back through to where it needs to "grow" but without picking up a bead.

Wrapped Bead

In this method (and the similar version described in "Bubbles"), seed beads are used to cover a larger core bead. Choose a bead for the core carefully - look for a nice round shape with a hole big enough to let your needle and thread go through lots of times, but not so big that seed beads will be sucked into it and clog it. Don't be tempted by too large a bead or your finished wrapped bead could be enormous!

If you are making a wrapped bead for the end of a toggle, use a thread attached to the bracelet to thread on the stem beads, drop the core bead down on to them and work the bead in situ. If you are making a "freestanding" bead, tie a long thread on to the core bead and have the thread exiting from the top of the bead. Hold the tail of thread as firmly as you can to stop the thread slipping around the core bead.

* Pick up as many seed beads as are needed to cover the side of the core from its top to its bottom holes. Making sure none of the seed beads slip inside the core bead, pass the needle up through it and pull tight. Repeat from *, but picking up one or two seed beads fewer, and lay the new group of beads alongside the first. Continue with alternating long and short lines until the core bead is covered. To get an absolutely smooth and even bead requires trial and error to get the number of beads right and, of course, practice makes perfect!

BUTTONS

Sometimes it is useful to have a button and loop fastening because, with the button sitting on top of the bracelet, there is no gap between the two ends of the beadwork when the loop goes over it. Here is one button you can make for your self and a couple of suggestion for decorating one from the assortment in your button box.

Spiral Button

The stitch used for this button is peyote in beads of three colours R, Y and B. Thread on 1R, 1Y and 1B and tie in a circle. Row 1: pass the needle through the R bead, pick up 1R (bead X) + 1Y and go through the Y bead in the circle. Pick up 1Y + 1B and go through the B bead in the circle. Pick up 1B + 1R and go through the R bead in the circle and bead X. Row 2: pick up 1R (bead Z) and go through the first Y bead picked up in Row 1. Continue around, picking up one bead and going through the next (beads to pick up: 2Y, 2B and 1R). Pass the needle through bead Z. Row 3: as for Row 2 except pick up 2 beads for every 1 used in Row 2.

If you want to make the button larger, work the next row with 1 bead going in between every bead picked up in Row 3; in subsequent rows, work increases when you judge it right - much will depend on the size of your beads and your tension.

You can of course make this button in just one colour, or start with 2 main and 1 contrasting for a swirling stripe.

Decorated Buttons

There are lots of ways to decorate buttons with beads, but here is just one to get you going: you will create many more!

Use seed beads in two colours: main (M) and contrast (C). Tie your thread to the centre of a button with four holes, with the knot underneath. * Bring your needle to the top of the button through one of the holes; pick up 1C bead and go back down the same hole. Repeat from * for the other three holes. You now have one bead sitting on top of each hole. Bring your needle to the top of the button through any of the holes and go through its bead. Now, pick up 1 M bead and go through the next bead around; repeat three times (this makes a little circle of beads). Either stop there, or # pick up 3 M beads and go through the nearest C bead again, pushing the little triangle of beads over so that it points to the button's outer edge; repeat from # three times. If you find that the beads don't fit in comfortably, try a slightly larger button or slightly smaller beads!

EDGINGS

Adding a decorative beaded edging to a piece of beadwork can, well - give it an "edge" over it's neighbours! There are many different styles and possibilities for you to explore, but here are two versions of a picot edging that are quick and simple to do. Once you have tried out the basics, experiment for yourself: try varying the number of beads; using different sizes of bead in the same edging; using two or more colours; working more rows on top........ And don't forget that you can use a beaded edging on your embroidery/soft furnishing/cross stitch and needlepoint projects too!

The directions are given in general terms so that you can adapt them to whatever type of stitch or project you are wanting to edge.

Triangular Picot Edge

Bring the needle out of an edge bead, thread on 3 beads (A, B & C), go back down into the next edge bead and out again through the next (for certain stitches this might be going under a loop of thread between beads) and then up through bead C. * Pick up 2 beads (B & C), go down into the next edge bead and out again through the next (or under loop as above) and up through bead C. Repeat from *.

Lacy Picot Edge

This is really an expanded version of the triangular picot edge, but what a different effect, especially if you use irregular "wobbly" beads (as we did in the Two Tone Triangles Bracelet). Work as for the triangular edge, but pick up 5 beads each time, go back down into your project making sure there is a wider gap so that your edging beads loop nicely, and bring the needle back up through the fifth bead.

STITCH INSTRUCTIONS

3-BEAD NETTING

Step 1: Thread on 27 beads and go back up through bead no. 21 to form a loop. Add three beads and go up through bead no. 17. Continue back to the top in this way. (Fig 1)

Step 2: To start the next row, add 1 extra bead (E) before picking up 3 beads and going through the centre bead of the last group you picked up in the previous row.   Continue to add 3 beads and go through the centre bead of the next group of 3 in the previous row. (Fig 2)

Repeat Step 2 until you have the required length.

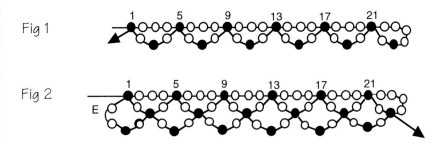

Fig 1

Fig 2

Shaping: the method of shaping will depend on its purpose - some trial and error called for!

To increase (edge or mid-row): you can switch to groups of 5 beads on some or all of the nets; or add a group of 5 in one row and work a 3 bead net into both the 2nd and 4th beads of that group on the next row.

To decrease: use only 1 bead instead of 3 in some or all of the nets; or pick up 5 beads and go through the next but one centre bead.

PEYOTE STITCH

Step 1: Thread on an even number of beads to give the desired width. Using an odd number causes complications so avoid it if you can. (Fig 1)

Step 2: Pick up one bead, miss a bead and put the needle back through the next bead (Fig 2); pull the thread tight. Repeat across the line (Fig 3)

Step 4: Work subsequent lines back and forth across the piece, continuing to pick up one bead at a time, putting the needle through the next "drop down" bead and thus filling the gaps between them (Fig 4).

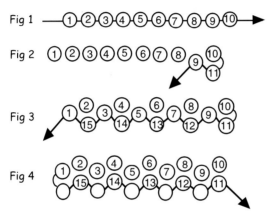

To increase: in mid-row, at the point of increase, add two beads instead of one and work into each of them on the next line. See "Ripple" for a way of increasing on the edge.

To decrease: in mid-row, simply go through two beads without picking up a bead to fill the gap between them and pull up tight. Work the next row as normal (Fig 5). See "Ripple" for a way of decreasing on the edge.

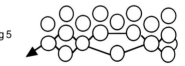

Peyote stitch can be varied by using a number of beads as a single bead. For example, 2-drop looks like this:

BRICK STITCH

Step 1: Foundation Row (also known as Ladder stitch) Start with two beads and join them together as shown in Fig 1. Make sure they stay side by side, not one on top of the other (not pulling too tight helps).

Step 2: Join on the third and fourth beads as shown in Fig 2 Repeat Step 2 until you have the desired width for your foundation row.

Step 3: Holding the line of beads with the thread on the left, pick up two beads and put the needle under the loops of thread which join the first two beads, and then up again through the second of the pair of beads you picked up. Make sure the bead on the edge is pushed over so that the beads sit side by side.

Pick up one bead and put the needle under the loops of thread which join the next two beads, and then up again through the new bead (Fig 3). Continue picking up one bead at a time until you get to the end of the row.

For every subsequent row, repeat step 3.

Using two beads at the beginning of each row means that thread does not show on the side of the work.

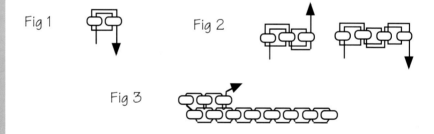

Fig 1

Fig 2

Fig 3

To increase: in mid-row, work two beads on to the same connecting loop; on the edge, add more beads using the foundation row.

To decrease: in mid-row, miss one of the connecting loops and pull tight; on the edge, put the needle under the second loop rather than the first.

Brick stitch can be varied by using a number of beads as a single bead. For example, 3-drop looks like this:

SQUARE STITCH

Begin by threading on beads for the desired width (here shown as eight). Then:

Step 1: Pick up one bead and "suspend" it from the last bead (Fig 1)
Step 2: Repeat this across the row, suspending a bead from each of the beads in the row above (Figs 2 & 3).
Step 3 (optional): Finally, reinforce the beading by going straight through the beads of both rows (Fig 4).
Repeat steps 1 and 2 (and 3 for a firmer fabric) until you have the length you require.

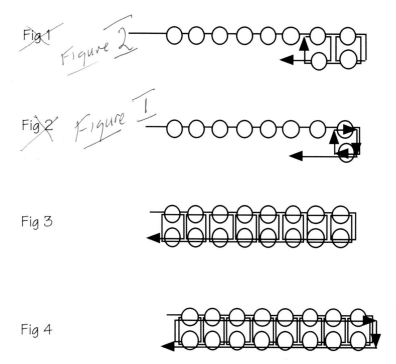

Fig 1

Figure 2

Fig 2

Figure 1

Fig 3

Fig 4

To increase: on the edge, pick up as many extra beads as you need, keep the thread taut and square stitch back along them and continue across the row. In mid row, simply pick up 2 beads on one row and work into both of them on the next.

To decrease: on the edge, simply turn and work back along the row without working the bead (or beads) on the outside edge. In mid-row, just skip a bead.

HERRINGBONE WEAVE

The foundation of herringbone weave makes two rows and starts with a multiple of 4 + 1 beads. The directions given here use 17 beads. To make the directions clear we have used black and white beads and we suggest you might like to practice with that combination a couple of times until you have got the hang of the stitch. In each case, the projects give you the colours to pick for the foundation row - you might find it useful to mark up the diagrams with the colours to help you see where you are going!

Foundation

Step 1: Thread on a stop bead. Using strongly contrasting colours, pick up 17 beads (Fig 1).
Step 2: Go back through the last light bead you picked up, miss two dark beads and go through the next light bead. (Fig 2)
Step 3: *Pick up two dark beads, go through the next light bead, miss two dark beads and go through the next light bead. Repeat from * twice more (Fig 3).

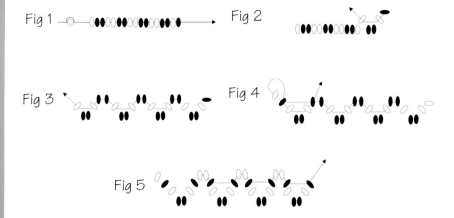

Pull the work up really tight and knot the two ends of thread together. (You'll need to slip off the stop bead to do this.) You will find that the dark beads picked up at the very beginning get pushed downwards and the new dark beads added in Step 3 sit on top of the light beads. Don't worry if it looks a little raggedy at this stage.

Row 1: Pick up one dark and one light bead, let them drop down to the work already in place and put the needle back down through the dark bead. Now go through the nearest bead of the last pair of dark beads picked up in the previous row (Fig 4).
* Pick up two light beads, go through the next two dark beads. Repeat from * twice more, thus placing pairs of light beads in between the pairs of dark beads of the previous row (Fig 5). Pull up tight.

Row 2: Pick up one light and one dark bead, let them drop down to the work already in place and put the needle back through the light bead. Now go through the nearest bead of the last pair of light beads picked up in the previous row. *Pick up two dark beads, go through the next two light beads. Repeat from * twice more, thus placing pairs of dark beads in between the pairs of light beads of the previous row. Pull up tight.

Repeat Rows 1 and 2 until you have the required length.

To increase: put in a pair of beads where normally you would go through without picking up at all.

To decrease: in mid-row, put in one bead instead of a pair, and miss it on the next row. On the edge, turn before you get to it.

Tips:

- ◆ turning the work over between rows can be helpful if you prefer to work in one direction only
- ◆ keep the work pulled up as tightly as you can

RIGHT ANGLE WEAVE

The directions given here are for single bead right angle weave. But, as the projects show, you can use more beads to make the sides of each "square" for a more open, lacy look. The diagrams show the thread making right angles to emphasise the sides of the "squares". But, in real life, the thread will form a curve between the beads.

The First Row

Pick up 4 beads and put the needle through the first bead again. Now put the needle down through the second bead you picked up. (Figs 1a and b)
* Pick up 3 beads and put the needle down through the bead the thread is coming out of. Now put the needle through the next two beads in the "square" you have just created. (Figs 2a and b)
Pick up 3 beads and put the needle up through the bead your thread is coming out of. Now put the needle through the next two beads in the square you have just created (Figs 3a and b)
Repeat from * until you have a strip of beadwork the length you want.

The Second Row

To turn and work back along the strip, put the needle through the bead at the bottom of the last square of beads. Pick up 3 beads and put the needle through the same bead again to form a new square. Finally, put the needle down through the bead on the left edge of the new square. (Fig 4)
* Pick up 2 beads and go through the bead at the bottom of the next square of beads in the strip. Then take the needle through the next three beads of the new square so that the thread exits on the left. (Fig 5)
Put the needle through the bead at the bottom of the next square of beads in the strip. Pick up 2 beads and put the needle up through the bead on the left edge of the previous square and then on through the next two beads in the new square so that the thread exits at the left. (Fig 6) Repeat from * all along the strip.

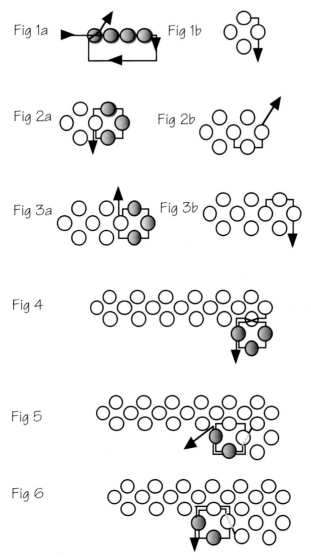

Fig 1a   Fig 1b

Fig 2a   Fig 2b

Fig 3a   Fig 3b

Fig 4

Fig 5

Fig 6

To increase: in mid row, pick up 3 beads instead of 2 and work a square on to both "bottom" beads on the next row. On the edge, make the first square of beads as in Fig 4 then needle round to the edge side and add another group of 3 beads. Turn, needle back through both squares and continue across the row as usual.

To decrease: in mid row, go through two "bottom" beads as though they were one. On the edge, needle back (keeping to the thread path) to exit from the bottom of the square at the decrease point.

3-BEAD NETTING

BRICK
STITCH

The
Beadworkers
Guild

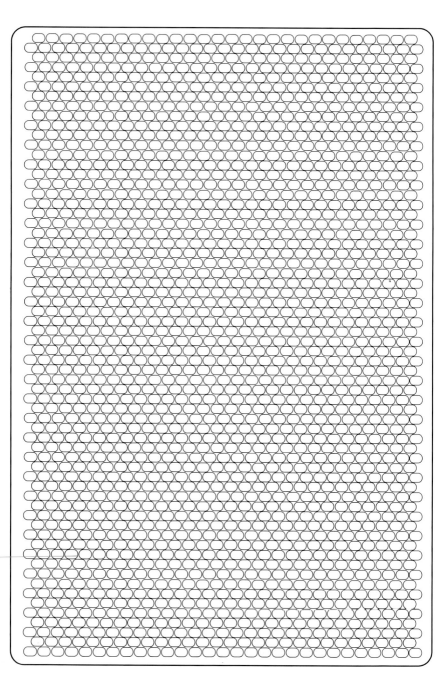

SQUARE
STITCH

The
Beadworkers
Guild

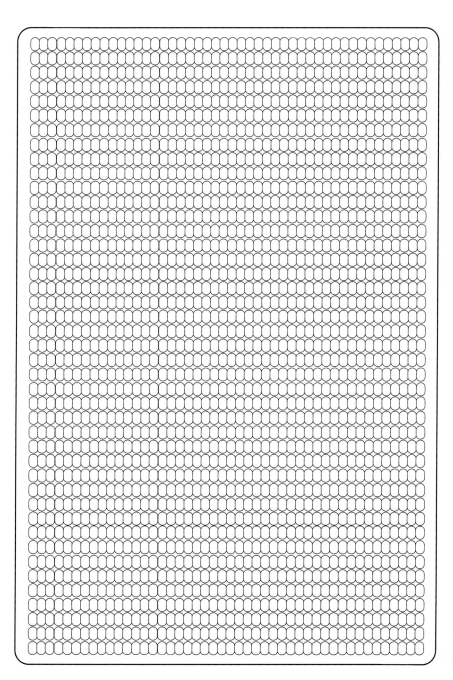

HERRINGBONE WEAVE

The
Beadworkers
Guild

RIGHT ANGLE WEAVE

The Beadworkers Guild

THE SUPPLIERS ◆ ◆ ◆

The following Bead Suppliers offer a 10% discount to Beadworkers Guild members who spend £40 or more in a single transaction:

The Bead Merchant

P.O. Box 5025, Coggeshall, Essex CO6 1HW
Tel 01376 563567 Fax 01376 563568
www.beadmerchant.co.uk

G.J.Beads

Court Arcade, The Wharf, St.Ives, Cornwall
Tel 01736 793886
www.gjbeads.co.uk

The London Bead Co

339 Kentish Town Road, London NW5 2TJ
Tel 0870 2032323 Fax 020 7284 2062

Sewing Seeds

38 Elmore House, Minet Road, London SW9 7TH
Tel 020 7737 1543

Spangles

1 Casburn Lane, Burwell, Cambs. CB5 0ED
Tel 01638 742024

Stitch'n'Craft

St.Martin's Sq, Gillingham, Dorset SP8 4DP
Tel 01747 821717
www.stitchncraft.co.uk

Additional suppliers can be found in the quarterly journal of
The Beadworkers Guild.